THIS BOOK BELONGS TO

_____

FOR THE KIDS WHO WANT TO WIN

ISBN: 9798894582221

PETE THE UNICORN BOUNCED WITH EXCITEMENT. TODAY WAS THE GREAT UNICORN RACE! THE FASTEST UNICORNS IN THE LAND WOULD COMPETE FOR THE GOLDEN TROPHY.

PETE DREAMED OF WINNING, BUT THERE WAS ONE BIG PROBLEM—HE WASN'T VERY FAST. NO MATTER HOW HARD HE TRIED, HE ALWAYS FELL BEHIND.

"I'LL NEVER WIN," PETE SIGHED. HIS BEST FRIEND, WHISKERS THE CAT, TWITCHED HER TAIL. "WINNING ISN'T JUST ABOUT SPEED," SHE SAID. "IT'S ABOUT STRATEGY!"

WHISKERS CLIMBED ONTO PETE'S BACK. "IF WE TRAIN THE SMART WAY, YOU MIGHT SURPRISE EVERYONE." PETE'S EARS PERKED UP. "OKAY! LET'S DO THIS."

THE RACE HAD BIG HURDLES, AND PETE ALWAYS KNOCKED THEM OVER. "YOU'RE JUMPING TOO SOON," WHISKERS OBSERVED.

"WAIT UNTIL YOU'RE CLOSER. THEN PUSH OFF STRONG!
" PETE FOCUSED, GALLOPED FORWARD, AND JUMPED!

HIS HOOVES SOARED OVER THE HURDLE. "YOU DID IT!" WHISKERS
CHEERED. PETE GRINNED. ONE CHALLENGE DOWN!

DURING RACES, PETE GOT DISTRACTED BY BUTTERFLIES, WAVING FLAGS, AND CHEERING CROWDS. "YOU LOSE TIME LOOKING AROUND," WHISKERS SAID.

SHE TIED A TINY FLAG TO PETE'S HORN. "KEEP YOUR
EYES ON THIS. IGNORE EVERYTHING ELSE."

PETE RAN A FULL LAP WITHOUT LOOKING AWAY. "GREAT JOB!"
WHISKERS PURRED. PETE FELT MORE CONFIDENT.

PETE'S LEGS GOT TIRED TOO QUICKLY. "YOU RUN TOO HARD AT THE START," WHISKERS POINTED OUT. "PACE YOURSELF."

THEY PRACTICED STEADY BREATHING AND SMOOTHER STRIDES.
PETE RAN WITHOUT STUMBLING OR SLOWING DOWN.

"MUCH BETTER," WHISKERS SAID. PETE FELT STRONGER.
"NOW, I HAVE A SECRET PLAN FOR RACE DAY..."

THE SUN ROSE OVER THE RACETRACK. THE FASTEST UNICORNS
LINED UP. PETE STOOD AMONG THEM, HEART POUNDING.

"ON YOUR MARKS... GET SET..." GO! THE RACE BEGAN!

DUST FLEW AS UNICORNS GALLOPED FORWARD. PETE SPRINTED, REMEMBERING HIS TRAINING. BUT THE OTHERS WERE STILL AHEAD.

THE UNICORNS' HOOVES KICKED UP THICK
DUST. PETE COULD BARELY SEE!

"JUMP LEFT, THEN RIGHT!" WHISKERS SHOUTED.
PETE ZIGZAGGED THROUGH THE DUST CLOUD.

HE COULD SEE THE TRACK AGAIN! HE WASN'T LAST ANYMORE!
WHISKERS CHEERED. "KEEP GOING!"

THE FINISH LINE WAS CLOSE! PETE
NEEDED SOMETHING EXTRA.

"NOW!" WHISKERS YELLED. PETE TOOK A DEEP
BREATH AND KICKED OFF THE GROUND!

INSTEAD OF RUNNING, PETE LEAPED FORWARD,
BOUNCING OFF HURDLES LIKE STEPPING STONES!

THE CROWD GASPED. NO UNICORN HAD
EVER RACED LIKE THIS BEFORE!

ONE HURDLE LEFT—PETE JUMPED HIGH AND
LANDED RIGHT BEHIND THE LEADERS!

HE WAS NECK AND NECK WITH THE FASTEST UNICORNS!

HIS HEART POUNDED. THIS WAS HIS LAST CHANCE.

PETE TOOK A DEEP BREATH, FOCUSED ON THE FINISH
LINE, AND RAN HARDER THAN EVER.

THE WIND RUSHED PAST HIM. HIS HOOVES
BARELY TOUCHED THE GROUND.

THE FINISH LINE WAS JUST AHEAD. HE WAS SO CLOSE!

THE OTHER UNICORNS PUSHED FORWARD,
BUT PETE WASN'T GIVING UP.

WHISKERS CLUNG TO HIS MANE. "GO, PETE, GO!"

PETE REMEMBERED HIS TRAINING. STEADY BREATH.
STRONG STRIDE. SMART MOVES.

HE GAVE ONE FINAL, POWERFUL LEAP!

HIS HOOVES HIT THE GROUND—RIGHT
AT THE FINISH LINE!

THE CROWD ERUPTED IN CHEERS. "PETE WINS!"
THE ANNOUNCER CALLED. HE HAD DONE IT!

PETE PANTED, STUNNED. HE HAD WON—NOT BY BEING
THE FASTEST, BUT BY BEING THE SMARTEST.

WHISKERS PURRED. "TOLD YOU SO." PETE
LAUGHED. "WE DID IT TOGETHER!"

THE GOLDEN TROPHY GLEAMED IN PETE'S HOOVES. HE HAD PROVED
THAT HARD WORK AND STRATEGY COULD BEAT PURE SPEED.

FROM THAT DAY ON, PETE NEVER DOUBTED HIMSELF.
HE WASN'T JUST A UNICORN—HE WAS A CHAMPION.

AND WITH WHISKERS BY HIS SIDE, PETE KNEW
HE COULD TACKLE ANY CHALLENGE.